This book is for those who know little or nothing about car repair but care about saving money. I have no plans to make you a car mechanic, just so you'll know the basics.

Research shows that most consumers feel out of control and vulnerable during the auto repair experience. This book will change some of that.

If your car doesn't start, I'll tell you what to do. If your car makes a funny noise, I'll tell you what to do. If your car smokes or rattles or stops, I'll tell you what to do. And when you take your car to a mechanic, I'll tell you what to ask and how to check the price.

In short, WHATEVER goes wrong with your car I'll tell you how to handle it in the smoothest, most effective, lease expensive manner.

# Save $$$ on
# Car Repairs

Everything You Ever Wanted to Ask Your Mechanic
But You Were Afraid He'd Laugh at You.

by
## Steve Gehrlein

with
## Cliff Evans

Swan Publishing

Authors: Steve Gehrlein with Cliff Evans
Editor: Pete Billac
Layout Artist: Sharon Davis
Cover Design: Bernadette and Dwight Berry
Photographers: Beverly Adams—Cover Photo
                        Toni Hanes—Inside Photos


Other Automotive Books Recommended:

How to Buy a New Car and Save Thou$ands
*by Cliff Evans*

Copyright @January 1999
Swan Publishing and Steve Gehrlein
Library of Congress Catalog Card #98-89422
ISBN# 0-943629-37-3

*Save $$$ on Car Repairs*, is available with quantity discounts through: Swan Publishing, 126 Live Oak, Alvin, TX 77511.
(281) 388-2547, Fax (281) 585-3738, e-mail: swanbooks@ghg.net, URL- http://www.swan-pub.com


Printed in the United States of America.

## Dedication

To Alton Huseman, 1917-1997, the father of my wife Judy, who became my father; I lost mine in childhood. His integrity and staunch morality became a beacon for me, and his love and support never faltered through many trials. To him, I dedicate this book. You are loved and missed.

# INTRODUCTION

This book will help you with your vehicle, whether it's a car, truck, van, bus, a 4x4, a motor home or any vehicle that is used in daily commutes. Even an airplane falls pretty much under this category. I say "car" or "automobile" throughout the book but know that if it has an engine or motor, if it requires steering, oil, gas, spark plugs and brakes. I'll answer questions you are afraid to ask your mechanic for fear they will laugh at you. But, I won't.

I'll try to make owning and driving a car the pleasurable experience it's supposed to be. I'll tell you how to spot "trouble signs" *BEFORE* you have to walk or go to the bank to pay for major repairs. I've been in the car repair business for more than 30 years and I know what I'm talking about. I'm assuming that those of you reading this book know absolutely nothing about "car trouble." With hundreds of different models, styles, types of engines and replacement parts on the many cars of today, it's almost impossible to know it all. But, I can tell you enough in this ten-dollar book which may save you much time, aggravation, and money.

Each Saturday and Sunday for the past six years, I've hosted a 2-hour radio show on KTSA in San Antonio (550 A.M. on your dial). I field up to 36 questions per show from callers spread over a 99-county area in South Texas. I have also owned Cambridge Auto Center, an auto repair shop, for more than 14 years.

I act as general manager and mechanic as well as perform *any* job that requires doing. It doesn't matter how demeaning it might seem, wiping up grease, sweeping the floor, and cleaning the rest rooms. The fact is, I like what I do. I also like people and I like to answer questions about their automobiles.

On my show, I answer questions about cars and trucks. Some of these questions are simple—to me—but they are real and important to you and I answer them all. I can almost see your head nodding back and forth when I hear you saying, "I didn't know that" or "Wow, **that's** what it is!"

I try to make my answers such that the average non-mechanically minded person can understand easily. I don't want to impress you or confuse you, just answer your questions in a manner that's easy to understand. Of course, when I get a question fielded by someone who *does* have extensive knowledge of auto repair, that's when I get the opportunity to show off—hopefully.

This book will be basic to some, but helpful to most. The greater majority of car owners, in my experience, know little or nothing about car repair. This book is meant to help you *prevent* needless repairs by doing proper maintenance, to save you money on the repairs you have to do, to give you an idea of what the costs are, and to help you choose a mechanic who will give you both, the best service, and price.

I guess I actually started in the auto repair business as a child. I would sit next to my dad, often wondering how cars worked and I listened to him talk of Model A's, T's and flathead V-8's. When I didn't understand something, I asked questions and often times I felt stupid.

Dad always said, "The only stupid question is the one you don't ask." I listened, learned, and listened some more and I became an automotive professional. There was a time when I didn't understand what a valve, crankshaft, carburetor or universal joint was.

I'm not going to try and make you a mechanic in this book; not everyone wants to be a mechanic. You won't even get your hands dirty, unless you *want* to.

Proper maintenance prevents most mechanical breakdowns. In 1997, according to the National Car Care Council, more than 25% failed their vehicle inspection because they needed engine oil, coolant or a new air filter.

In this book, I will give you the answers to how to "properly maintain" your automobile as well as some insight in the auto repair industry. It *will* help you minimize your automotive expenses. You will learn how to determine a course of action and how to deal with auto repair people and learn how to get it *right the first time* **when** your vehicle breaks. It's as certain to eventually happen as death and taxes. Last year 28% of the motorists surveyed had an automobile break-down.

By buying this book, you have taken the first step to becoming much happier with your automobile through improved performance, lower repair cost, greater dependability, better economy and, most of all, safety for you, your family and all of the other drivers on the road. ***Good luck!***

*Steve Gehrlein*

# Table of Contents

# Chapter 1

# What the Salesman Didn't Tell You

Welcome to THE AUTOMOTIVE SHOW on 550 KTSA. I'm your host, Steve Gehrlein from Cambridge Auto Center in San Antonio. Let's punch up line number one. What is your question?

## PM: WHAT IS IT AND WHAT DOES IT MEAN?

**PM** means **PREVENTIVE MAINTENANCE**. It is the upkeep at predetermined mileage and time intervals to keep your automobile running at its peak performance. All cars require PM no matter how much they cost. I have seen owners of Mercedes Benz come to my repair shop and cry when they realize that their 45-thousand-mile auto needs necessary and costly repair that an overzealous salesman failed to tell them about at the time of purchase. I can't count the number of times drivers have told me, "Nobody ever told me I had to do *that*!"

A friend of mine, now a used car dealer, once told me that it always amazed him how often the owner of a car would go to great lengths to give him the **owner's manuals** when selling their cars to him.

He went on to say he frequently asked them if they had ever actually *read* it. The incredible thing was that more than nine out of 10 of them quickly said, "**NO**."

Don't smile or laugh. Have **you** ever read **your** owner's manual? I'll bet you pick it up only when some little light comes on and you need to find out what it means or to set those radio buttons on the station of your choice. I'm right, aren't I? I'm not laughing at you; most people do the same thing. Yes, woefully, most people spend less time reading the owner's manuals for their $20,000, $30,000 & *UP* automobiles than they do reading the owner's manual for a $150 video cassette recorder.

## OWNER'S MANUAL

The owner's manual is packed full of useful information specific to your automobile that can't be found anywhere else. As a rule, the manufacturers specifically designed these manuals to be concise, yet simplified, so a relative *dummy* can be made aware of the safest operation of all of the features of their automobile. I am not sure if they are trying to be helpful, reduce warranty repair costs, or just avoid lawsuits. It's probably all of the above.

Some of the stuff is really basic but, dad once told me, "It's what you learn *after* you know it all that counts." I knew one person that drove a '72 Ford Thunderbird with the steering wheel in the *top tilt position* for years because he didn't know it had **tilt steering,** *until I got in his car and moved it!* He had never really liked the car because the wheel was so uncomfortable and he had to drive with his elbows high in the air. Imagine his surprise when I reached over and gently pushed the turn signal indicator toward the dash. When the wheel tilted, his eyes popped wide open and suddenly he had an entirely different, **comfortable** automobile that he LOVED. What he should have done when he first got his car was *READ HIS OWNER'S MANUAL.*

The manual not only has descriptions of the features of your car with drawings and pictures, but there is also a **maintenance schedule** in there. Maintenance is paramount to the longevity of your car. I call it "**PM**." I don't mean the time of day. It is called *PREVENTIVE MAINTENANCE.*

PM keeps your automobile running longer because you adjust or replace components that change or wear during operation before they fail or cause a failure. I consider oils, grease and other fluids to be essential components of your car.

One, for example, gasoline (or diesel) is a component that requires PM. If you don't put some in your tank before you run out, your car will stop and not run until you do. You **prevent** running out of gas by filling up before it's empty. Simple, I know, but we've all seen people walking along the road with a gas can in their hands headed for the nearest service station.

Yet, motorists try to *test* the car and see how far they can drive on empty before the engine stutters and stops. READ THE MANUAL! It tells what your reserve is. Better yet, when your gas gauge gets to **half** empty fill up. So what if it's two cents a gallon more at this station, it's still less expense (certainly less trouble) than having to walk, or try to hitch a ride, then buy a gas can and try to start your car.

If your car (or truck) is diesel powered, running out of fuel can be extremely expensive. Most diesels must have the air bled from the fuel lines after one has run empty. Fuel pump damage could result as well as injector damage.

It's the same with oil, filters, transmission fluid, coolant, hoses, belts, tires, timing belts, etc.

Your owner's manual has the **specific** items that need PM and the intervals that they need to be done. You will notice that there are two different classifications of the maintenance schedule.

The first is "normal use." For the life of me, I don't know what "normal" is. But, it certainly isn't in any part of Texas or anywhere else that I know of. I guess if you only drove your car between 7:00 P.M. and 8:00 P.M. in the Spring and Fall, your car might actually fit the "normal" classification.

The second is "severe duty." This is for vehicles driven in ambient temperatures either above 80° or below 32° or vehicles driven in "*stop and go*" traffic. This sounds more "normal" than "severe" to me.

I recommend using the "severe duty schedule" in all cases to prevent failures. It will require maintenance more often, but I have never heard of a vehicle that had been damaged by maintaining it too much.

Indulge me if you will, and fold the corner of this page over and get your owner's manual and read it right now. Do it, please. It's a part of this book. You'll discover wonders in it. Think of it as an extra *free chapter* of this book. There might be a test later, so be sure to have it handy. Sure, it can be an open book test. I just want to save you time, aggravation and money.

Fewer than three our of every five vehicles in the U.S. were tuned up last year although three of every four owners said they are aware of their car's recommended maintenance schedule according to the American Automobile Association.

Stop right now and get your owner's manual out of your glove compartment. If you haven't read it before, do it now, please.

---

**Misconception: In the past seven years health services have increased 45%, dental services 52% and auto service but 30%.**

# Chapter 2

# Preventive Maintenance

The following PM's are ideas taken from major computer repair systems used by repair professionals. They are frequently referred to as, "Recommended Maintenance Items." Read on and you'll see the importance of properly maintaining your car.

Remember, your automobile is usually the **second** most important and expensive thing that you own; your house is usually the first. Your auto, while only coming in a *close* second on your most expensive list, does many things your home can't do. The vehicle you drive takes you everywhere; to work, school, church, the grocery store and the all-important mall adventure.

We actually depend on it to start, run, play music, give us the news, cool us, warm us and jump over or drive through different obstacles. All this we expect while delivering up to 40 mpg (miles per gallon) at 70 mph (miles per hour). While all these things are going on, we are driving in zero degree weather to 128° temperatures and are in everything from two feet of snow to 18 inches of water. This is what we ask of our automobiles.

The average automobile consists of more than 17,000 different parts and it, is completely assembled at a factory in less than 40 hours. The dealer knocks the dust off, vacuums it out and hands you the keys. For the next couple of 100,000 miles or so, you expect to hop in, *fasten your seatbelts*, turn the key, *vvvrrrrooommm*, and *GO!* Amazingly enough, it actually does happen (most of the time).

**What is the most important maintenance I can do on my car?**

**CHANGE OIL REGULARLY!** Also get a chassis lube and the tire pressures checked. Be sure to ask your mechanic to give it a quick safety check and to look for potentially dangerous concerns. Since people's lives are so hectic, some folks depend on oil change specialty shops to do this dirty, thankless work. DON'T LET THESE PEOPLE BE THE ONLY ONES TO CHECK YOUR OIL!

With the advent of grocery store gas stations, the need to check your oil is up to usually up to you. Don't be fooled by the cute 18-year-old high school kid shouting out orders to a fellow 18-year-old in the grease pit. **Ask them** what oil *type* and *weight* of the oil they are putting in your auto. ***Ask them*** if the oil is **100% new oil** or is it 50% recycled? Recycled oil is **used oil** sold as new oil at some discount outlets. It is allowed under federal law.

And don't let that 18-year-old tell you that you don't have to change the oil that much. Not changing the oil often could **void** your warranty.

A warranty might say to change the oil under "normal conditions" at 7,500 miles, but early changes will **not** void the warranty unlike **not** changing the oil will. That $5,000 engine in your Toyota Camry is depending on you to service the oil at **3,000** mile intervals. Don't let it down.

A good rule of thumb is an oil CHANGE *each* 3,000 miles, and an oil level CHECK every two tanks of gas (or 600 miles). If the level is DOWN one quart or more in two tanks of gas, you've got a major leak or an oil-burning problem in the engine.

Make sure a **new oil FILTER** is put on with every oil change. It will add miles to your vehicle by removing all the abrasive deposits that are left in the old filter that could re-enter your crankcase. Severe damage could result from over filling your crankcase with oil. It is extremely important to check your oil carefully and determine within the nearest quart how much is needed. Do not add oil until it is exactly at or below the "add one quart" mark! *Almost* a quart low will not hurt anything. Over filling could cause damage.

Once you locate your dipstick, be sure you have waited at least five minutes after turning off your engine. The oil has been pumped up all over the internal components of the engine and needs time to completely drain back down to the oil pan.

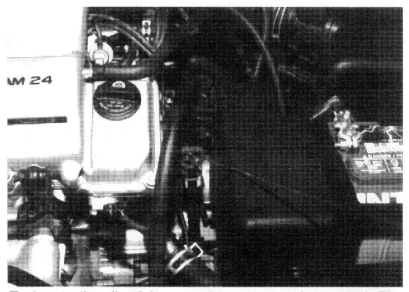

*To locate the dipstick, consult your owner's manual. The handle of the dipstick will be round shaped to make it easy to pull and it will usually be colored yellow, red or blue to contrast with the surrounding components.*

Waiting will also allow the motor to cool, making the oil level check a bit more comfortable. Have a disposable rag or paper towel ready to use to wipe off the dipstick. You might use it like a potholder on the dipstick handle, if you can't wait for the engine to cool.

*Slowly* pull the dipstick out taking note of where it came from. That little hole will be hard to see when you reinsert the dipstick if you don't remember where it is. Also, don't get any dirt on the dipstick. It could possibly cause eventual internal damage to your automobile's very expensive engine.

*Slowly pull the dipstick (be sure to look at where the little hole is as you pull it out), wipe it off, put it back in (all the way) and pull it out again to get an accurate reading.*

Wipe the dipstick *clean* and reinsert it as far as it will go. Slowly remove it again and observe the oil on the end of the stick.

Most dipsticks are flat with hash marks indicating a range of "safe" operation. A few are merely round rods with scored marks. Others are notched on their side. If your oil level is below the "add one quart" mark, you need to add one quart and check again. Be sure to give the oil ample time to fully drain back down to the crankcase after adding the oil.

*Wipe the dipstick off with a clean rag.*
***KEEP DIRT OFF THE DIPSTICK!***

***NEVER, NEVER OVERFILL THE OIL!*** If you accidently overfill it, you will have to remove the drain plug and drain some out before you start your engine! Overfilled crankcases will cause the oil seals to blow out and your engine will leak oil constantly or worse. Also, if you do drain some out, dispose of it properly. Do not pour it back in. It could get contaminated from the bottom of the oil pan. Spend a few dollars and get some new oil. If you find you are more than a quart low, increase the frequency of the oil level check.

If the consumption is much more than a quart every 800 miles, you need some repairs as soon as possible. Report the miles per quart used to a shop.

*Some dipsticks are "notched" to indicate the level of your engine oil, as shown.*

One last note about checking your oil, you can get a relative reading of the condition of your engine and motor oil by inspecting the oil on the dipstick. If you just changed your oil it will be clear, if you haven't started your vehicle yet. If you have, it may already appear a little dirty. This is usually normal.

After a few hundred miles, the oil will appear dark; no need to worry. If the oil is chocolate brown and milky-looking, there is water in it and *serious* engine problems are imminent.

*When adding oil, take care not to spill any on the outside of the engine. Use a funnel if necessary. Oil in contact with hot engine components could easily ignite and cause an engine compartment fire!* ***Very Dangerous!***

Get to a repair shop ASAP! Any alternative would not be to your liking! Please, follow the advice in this book.

Should your oil be very black and have a tar-like appearance, you haven't been changing your oil at proper intervals. You should have a repair professional flush your crankcase to try to save your engine. It may not be possible.

If your oil feels "gritty" or you can see metallic particles on your finger, an internal component is in the process of failing. Timely repair might reduce the overall cost of repair.

If your oil has a strong burned smell, it has been "cooked" from overheating and a crankcase flush is in order. If you have changed your oil regularly and you haven't waited too long, this might save your engine.

I hope I didn't scare you. I don't mean to, but with a little care, you can substantially increase the intervals between trips to the repair shop. Millions of people maintain their own engine oil and I'm sure you can too!

## TIRES

Tires are a constant source of trouble for the average person. You need to look at the tire as an expensive balloon because many things can cause it to leak or blow out.

Tires have several *DOT* (means Department of

Transportation) ratings that, once understood, makes sense on the safety and performance rating of your vehicle.

Buy a tire with a *minimum of a 4-ply rating* on the tread and inflate it **EXACTLY** to the **TIRE** *(not the auto)* **MANUFACTURER'S** pressure rating. The tire company spent years of research to figure out the pressure level; the auto manufacturer merely puts these tires on.

**PROPER INFLATION** will give you longer tread life, better gas mileage, and better handling. A **44-lb.** pressure-rated tire that has **32-lbs.** of pressure in it will soften the ride, but it wears out the outside tread of the tire sooner and may create handling problems.

And a **44-lb.** tire pressure in a tire rated at **32-lbs.** will wear out the center of the tread and is likely to blow out (*EXPLODE*) without warning. Proper inflation is necessary to take full advantage of the safety design of the tire. Your tires are your ONLY link to the road surface. No traction, no stopping until some immobile object stops you. Be safe!

Have the **ROTATION and BALANCING** of these tires done at least every **8,000 to 10,000** miles. It lengthens the tire's life considerably. I've heard as much as 50% of the tire life can be recovered by proper rotation and balancing. Some people rotate every 3,000 miles to avoid uneven wear problems. It usually cost less than $20.00 and could make a big difference in your tire life. Tires are balanced to eliminate harmonic vibrations and preserve tread life.

When you **buy** tires, a cheaper tire does not mean a long-lasting tire. Tires that are cheap are often referred to as *May Pop* tires. They may pop now or may pop later. Spend your money wisely.

I prefer a *Michelin* radial for all vehicles since their tires usually are among the top three best—rated. Of course, Uniroyal, General, Goodyear, Pirelli, Firestone, Bridgestone, and the many other major brands make a high quality premium tire. There are as many good brands of tires as bad ones. Remember, *cheap* and *quality* do not go together.

Buy a good **tire gauge** and check your tires every month. A *Milton* 50 lb. gauge will do you a good job for several years. Don't drop the gauge or use it as a pry bar since the accuracy will then be in question.

A FRONT-END ALIGNMENT is a good idea every six months also. If you hit a curb or pothole and are jolted really hard, get another alignment as soon as possible. Failure to do so will result in premature tire wear, tie-rod end damage and potential loss of control.

## BRAKES

An 8,000 lb. 4X4 Suburban driven at high speed, loaded and towing a trailer, could normally wear out front brakes at 12,000 mile intervals. A small GS 300 Lexus, driven in town, may wear out 60,000 mile brakes in as few as 40,000 miles. The traveling salesman in a Chevy Caprice Classic on the interstate may not need brakes for more than 100,000 miles. Whatever vehicle you drive, your individual driving habits could lengthen or shorten the miles between brake jobs substantially.

As cars have gotten smaller the role of brakes has increased. As vehicles got faster and more like race cars, the need for **ABS** (anti-lock brake system) brakes was created. To keep your brakes in good working order you must learn certain details.

For example, the noise produced by brakes may be barely noticeable. If your brakes begin to squeal, even a bit, have them looked at. *CERTAINLY*, if they grind, jerk, pull, leak fluid, or don't stop like they should, you are undoubtedly in trouble. **Get them fixed immediately.** If you don't care about your life, care about mine. I'm probably driving the same roads you're driving.

The most often checked items in my shop are brakes and the parts that make up the hardware of the hydraulic brake system. Over the years brakes have changed from mechanical brake systems to hydraulic (and later vacuum-assisted) to make the brakes easier to apply.

All these different systems offer distinctive qualities that are good or bad, but they all do one thing very well, that is, **they stop your vehicle**. The basic operating principle of brakes is that friction pads are pressed against rotating steel rotors or brake drums when pedal pressure is applied thereby impeding their rotation. This action slows or stops your car or truck.

The service of your brakes is critical and a complete check out of the brakes at least **once a year** is important. If you discover that brakes need to be relined, make sure you go to a shop that uses quality pads and brake shoes. I'm not knocking on the heads of these quick-fix brake places. The editor of this book has a Mercedes. His brakes began to squeal so he drove it into the first place he could find, a fix-it-while-you-wait so-called *specialty* spot.

He went back and forth FIVE times and his brakes continued to squeal. He drove a total of 250 miles and waited more than 15 hours in the shop waiting area—and the brakes STILL squealed.

The store manager was really nice, they had just opened this franchise store, they put in this and that, they greased it, oiled it, changed pads, tightened something else, but within a day or two the brakes were again making noise.

He finally took it to a *real* Mercedes mechanic who put in **Mercedes pads** and it was fixed. What happened is that this shop wanted to save a few DOLLARS and put in pads that were $12 instead of $19. Stupid, huh?

The fact is, these friction pads are **designed** to wear out. The average life for brake pads is as varying as the different vehicles and types of drivers there are on the roads today. If you apply the brakes easily, they will last longer. If you jam on them hard, they won't last very long at all. If you speed to a stop sign then slam on the brakes, of course they will wear out faster.

When you have your brakes checked, they will make sure the hydraulic parts are not leaking or very rusty. Make sure the drums or rotors are turned twice on a brake lathe. If this work is done properly, the brakes will not make noise and they will stop smoothly without pulling left or right.

If the car has an ABS (anti-lock brake system), make certain the repair shop facility services this system with either an *OTC monitor 4,000, Snap-On Scanner, or the manufacturer's special diagnostic computer designed for your vehicle* to reset and purge the ABS system's computer. Don't take chances with your brakes.

## TUNE-UP

The way an engine runs and pulls your vehicle down the road is all based on how well the engine can do its job. A poorly maintained engine with old tired spark plugs pollutes the air as much as 30 new, well tuned, engines. The costs of fuel and dependability all increase or decrease with the performance of the engine. What we once referred to as a **tune-up** is now called a **performance enhancement**.

Late model cars are commonly *multi-port fuel*

*injected* with an *on board computer* called an ECM (electronic control module). Automotive electronics began in earlier model vehicles with an electronic carburetor. Around 1980, GM started the trend that led to the conversion to TBI (throttle body injection) in 1987. Ford started in 1983 and reached the multi-port fuel injected stage in about 1988. All domestic cars and light trucks are now ECM-COMPUTER controlled systems. ECM *does* lengthen the interval between necessary tuneups.

Let's set the record straight. A service center that offers a $50 tune-up is only changing spark plugs. For $50, how could they replace a $30 distributor cap, a $10 fuel filter, eight $3 spark plugs, and a $15 air filter and that's not even counting the labor?

Most dealerships will advertise a list of the different components of a tune-up and if all the old parts are added up, they charge about $300 for a *performance enhancement*. If you think this is a misleading marketing tool, you are right. A quality independent shop like mine will quote you a good tune-up with original quality parts, usually from the original manufacturer, for less than the listed services at many dealerships. Fact!

You see, today, some slick marketing man has taken the tune-up of 10 years ago and stripped it into eight or 10 services that cost more—separately—than when lumped together. Yet, people believe that the dealership is their friend and has their best interest at heart. *Hey*, if you have the money, take your vehicle to a franchise dealership, they'll usually do it right, but it *WILL* cost you a little extra.

These places are mostly for those who have "made it" and don't care about money, those with cars that are still under warranty, or those who don't know any better. But, they *do* spoil you. You'll meet a service manager with a clean uniform, maybe a spiffy bow tie, and a shiny aluminum pad to write up the order. They will escort you to their waiting room with color TV and offer you Cappuccino. And they will repair your vehicle and guarantee the work. You'll pay for it though. And why not? You've earned it. You deserve it.

But for working stiffs, or those who have limited funds, try an independent shop that you trust. Have someone follow you there to give you a ride home; chances are they won't have a *loner*. Then, relax. You'll save money—guaranteed.

You need to tune-up your vehicle every 30,000 miles and change the fuel filter each 15,000 to 20,000 miles. This reason is, fuel is stored in a tank buried underground which is not a clean, dry place. Fuel will dissolve almost everything it comes in contact with, and fuel gets dirty and usually has some moisture in it; in some areas, large amounts of water.

Too, your fuel *filter* will get dirty sooner or later which will cause your injectors to get dirty and cease to function properly. The result is poor fuel economy and poor performance. If your vehicle is equipped with a carburetor, a dirty fuel filter will eventually cause the vehicle to die or stop running due to lack of sufficient fuel flow.

I recommend that you NOT believe a vehicle can go 100,000 miles between tuneups, no matter *who* tells you it will. Just because it *runs* doesn't mean that it is running efficiently. You need a tune-up every 30,000 miles. Again, that is my opinion. There are new cars with specially designed engines (such as the Cadillac Northstar system) that the manufacturers swear can run 100,000 miles between tuneups (and a few more vehicles with similar claims). For most cars, go by my 30,000-mile rule.

Everybody's definition of a tune-up is different. If you don't consider a fuel filter, PCV valve, spark plug wires, air filter or distributor cap part of a tune-up then YES, you can go 100,000 miles between tuneups.

The problem with 100,000 mile tune-up intervals is that these items wear out no matter how well or by whom they were made. The fuel filter and misfiring spark plug wires can cause other damage to very expensive sensors and, in some cases, may lead to computer failures.

My word to you is to take the time to tuneup your engine to avoid creating even larger repairs that definitely cost MORE than would a 30,000 mile check up and tuneup.

## TRANSMISSIONS

This is the place where all the horsepower your vehicle creates is turned into manageable power at your wheels. A transmission is the big aluminum thing right behind your engine. What a misunderstood object this is. Whether it is a five-speed standard or a fully electronic overdrive automatic transmission, it can be the object of much pain and suffering. If you, as a consumer, must go to that dark hole in life called the transmission repair shop, know that it translates into big bucks.

Let this sink in—please. If you take your car to a shop that only repairs **one part** of the car, chances are they will "find" something wrong with *that* part. I learned a long time ago to be good at *all* repairs and not to specialize in only one area of a car.

An automatic transmission is very complex and should be approached with utmost care. A small dark shop with older cars around being repaired is not where you want to take a 1995 Nissan Pathfinder with a $4,500 6-speed automatic transmission. Let your first impression guide you and if it says *beware*, then please beware! You know how often that little voice inside is right, don't you?

Remember my editor with the Mercedes brake problems? He stopped in a small repair shop for them to look at his a/c compressor; he felt the air was a bit warmer than it should have been.

"The *mechanic* lifted the hood and looked to the right side of the engine, then to the left, then stooped down to look *under* something. He said he couldn't find the compressor. I smiled, nudged him back, closed the hood and drove off."

His non-mechanical mind had reasoned that if the guy didn't know WHERE the compressor was, chances are he certainly would not know how to fix it. Guess the guy's not that dumb after all.

With *any* shop, if they don't have the *latest* equipment needed for today's transmissions, you should not let them work on your transmission. Don't be afraid to ask if they have the latest high tech computerized diagnostic machines. And, if the manager even hesitates, he's probably lying.

Your vehicle's automatic transmission should be serviced every 25,000 to 30,000 miles. This includes flushing the transmission, installing a new filter, pan gasket and replacing the transmission fluid. BMW and several other companies say you don't have to service them that often. Perhaps, but I'm telling you that it is your money and the automatic transmission is the second most costly component on that vehicle.

*A hundred bucks of prevention is worth $3,000 of cure.* You heard the saying, *"Pay me now or pay me later?"* Trust the fact, the "pay me later" bill is at least 30 times more.

If you tow or drive over very hot territory, like South Texas or Death Valley, the fluid suffers a breakdown that damages the inside of the automatic transmission. The fluid is actually a *paraffin-based* product that not only acts like a hydraulic fluid but also as a friction modifier to help the clutches grab and efficiently transfer power to the rear wheels. Like the wax on a candle, the fluid will burn if excessive heat is present. Once the fluid burns, the internal components become "glazed" and appear like they are covered with scorched varnish. Total loss of the transmission of power is imminent.

If you listen to some manufacturer's claims that their automatic transmissions don't require regular servicing, you will *eventually* change your fluid when you have to **replace the transmission** at a cost of several thousands of dollars. Not to mention the time you won't have a vehicle to drive.

## GENERAL CHECK UP

If you read the owners manual, it might have told some you what I'm telling you. A good rule is to service your vehicle according to the charts in the owner's manuals—with some exceptions, all of which I noted and told you why.

✔ *Change your oil each 3,000 miles. Or, in extreme conditions like high temperatures, stop and go traffic, or long drives at high speed, you should change your oil at 2,000 to 2,500 mile intervals. These additional oil changes are cheaper than a $2,500-$4,000 engine replacement.*

✔ Service your transmission every 25,000 to 30,000 miles. Cut this in half if you're towing, or driving fast in high temperatures (average temps around 100°F for over a week or two).

✔ Keep your tires inflated to tire specifications. Rotate and balance them every 8,000 to 10,000 miles. If you hit a curb or a pot hole hard, have your alignment checked before you wear out your tires.

✔ Brakes need to be inspected each year, or every 25,000 miles, or every third tire rotation. You decide which.

✔ Get a tune-up every 25,000-30,000 miles or keep a log of gas mileage usage. When fuel economy drops two tanks in a row, get the vehicle tuned up.

✔ Change your wiper blades each year. Wipe them clean each time you wash your car. They collect grease and sand that will scratch your windshield. Check your washer fluid also.

✔ Lights should be checked once a month. Replace all lights that are out, because they were put there for a reason; **safety!**

✔ Air filters should be changed as often as needed due to conditions and driving styles. Occasionally check them by lightly tapping them on your driveway. If there is an excess accumulation of grit on your driveway where you tapped, replace the filter.

✔ Wax your car (or have it done professionally) every six months to a year with a good sun screen wax. The surface of your car oxidizes in the sun, snow and rain, not to mention industrial fallout and acid rain. It costs much less to replace the coat of wax than to have it repainted.

✔ Batteries should be serviced at least once a month. Try to buy a battery with **removable** caps so you can keep the water level up. Be sure you use **distilled** water, not tap water or mineral water or any other of those fancy waters on the grocery store shelf. Use the 39¢ per gallon "distilled" water. Unless you have a **sealed gel battery**, the battery has a sulfuric acid and water electrolyte. The battery off-gasses and the electrolyte evaporates even on so-called "maintenance free" batteries.

---

*You don't have to be a mechanic to recognize many problems with your vehicle!*

# Chapter 3

# Diagnosing a Problem

Even the best maintained car will eventually break. One of the most frustrating things an auto owner has to deal with is the diagnosis of a problem with their car.

You know how your car normally sounds and feels when you start it and drive it. When you notice a change, there is always a cause. It's usually the failure of some component.

Have you ever taken your car to a shop or dealership and told the service advisor (that's what they like to be called), "My car is making a funny noise and it seems to be coming from under the hood." Or, "It just doesn't seem to want to go after I stop?" They take your car and your ride takes you back to work.

Later the service advisor calls and says, "You need an alternator belt, a lower radiator hose, spark plugs and wires with a minor tuneup. The total will be $243.90 plus tax. It should be ready tomorrow morning if you approve."

You approve the charges and are relieved knowing your car will be "*right*" tomorrow.

You assume your car will be fixed. The next day

you get a ride to work and then to the shop to pick up your car. You pay your bill, get in your car and the noise is **still there**!

You return to the shop. The *advisor* states, "You see, under the space I wrote, *"check noise under hood,"* the technician wrote, *"NPF."* The items we discussed, that you approved, were listed by our computer as recommended maintenance items based on the mileage of your vehicle."

"So what the heck is *NPF?*" you ask, trying to restrain yourself. You are then told casually, "No Problem Found!" Two Hundred Forty Three Dollars of your hard-earned money and it ain't fixed yet!

The following pages will teach you how to diagnose and check out your vehicle thoroughly without any mechanical aptitude at all. I will also teach you how to *communicate* with a repair professional so you get it fixed right the first time.

As I said before, you know how your car usually sounds and feels when you start it and drive it. Try to improve your awareness of your machine. Know what it sounds like when it's running right.

When you notice something different about your vehicle, if it is not a complete breakdown, figure out how to duplicate the noise, rattle, surge, if it hesitates or dies, etc. See if you can *identify* where it is coming from within a two or three-foot range. Don't worry about what the name of the part is. Concentrate on how to best describe a bang, pop, rattle, creak, groan, squeal, chirp, grind, roar, surge, stumble, jerk, click, pull, or any number of unspellable glottal noises humans can make imitating a vehicle's malfunction. Practice making them. But know this, if *you* can't write it on paper, it probably won't get fixed

Unless you are dealing with a one-man shop, odds are you may never see the guy who actually *WORKS* on your car. Usually, a service advisor takes your comments about your car one at a time, and writes his translation in a little box. Some shops are now computerized, so he types it on a keyboard. This, at least, eliminates the common problem of poor handwriting.

This is called a "RO," Repair Order. Usually, it is then sent to a person called a "dispatcher." The dispatcher posts the RO number to his dispatch sheet where he has listed the technicians by their specialty. For each concern listed, the dispatcher interprets which area of specialty to send the car.

As a technician (this is what mechanics like to be called) is available, the dispatcher tears off the last of four carbon copies, which is a cardboard copy. One of the other copies is sent to the parts dispatcher.

The technician has to interpret this RO which is barely legible, not in full sentences, and vague at best. This is his first *tool* to repair your vehicle.

Write down a short, concise description of what you want done in an itemized list. You might consider keeping a note pad in your car to log details. Be sure to include information necessary to duplicate your concern or what it takes to "make it do it again."

Include statements like, ". . . at 30 MPH while lightly braking and turning left going up an incline."

Do whatever it takes to communicate, in writing, **EXACTLY** what you think is happening with your car to a person who may not be an English major at The University of Texas. If I said simple but detailed, you'd say I was nuts. This reminds me of what the parts guy said when I returned a wrong part, "It's the same, only different." It's your downtime and your money you are protecting so, be precise. We'll discuss what to do when you get the *"ESTIMATE"* call in the next chapter.

For now, I want to cover how you should "Check Out" your vehicle occasionally and I'll include some common problems to be on the lookout for.

## GENERAL VEHICLE CHECK-OUT PROCEDURE

Go to your car, get in the driver's seat, put the key in the ignition and turn. *Click!* The dome light goes dim . . . and bright again as you release the key to try again . . . *click! Cllllliiiiiiiicccccckkkk!* Nothing but a few expletives deleted.

A dead battery is always a bad sign. More often than not, a bad battery is only an indication of other problems. A difficult or slow to start vehicle will, more than likely, not start at the worst possible time. If the starter grinds or sounds funny, you might make note.

There should be no knocking noises on start up even if they go away after it warms (unless it's a diesel). You may hear the fuel injectors clicking on many vehicles; they will be slightly louder than faint and will usually be consistent at idle. This is normal.

If you sit in the driver's seat with the door open, hood up and all brakes on (including the parking brake), put the transmission in *drive* and slowly raise the engine speed slightly above idle. An engine with a rod or main bearing problem will usually begin to knock. It will sound like a metallic hammering, increasing as you increase engine speed. Do not get over-zealous doing this or you could damage motor mounts with too much engine RPM.

Visually observe the engine while performing this test. It should rise slightly with the torque but it should not jump or rise much, as this would be an indication of broken motor mounts. It is best to seek repair immediately on a vehicle with any of these problems.

If so equipped, turn on the air conditioner. The compressor will click and make a slight noise when running. The emphasis is on *slight*, not loud knocking. The belt should not *squeal*, this is an indication of a compressor that may quit soon. The vents should begin to cool the air soon. There should be no "*smoke*" or extremely "*cold looking*" air coming from the vents. This is an indication of a low refrigerant condition. It only gets low from a leak. Contrary to popular belief, an air conditioner doesn't *consume* refrigerant; it shouldn't leak. Get it repaired before you damage your compressor.

It is a good idea to test all modes of the heating and air conditioning system. Let the heater get hot, and the air conditioner get cold, regardless of what the temperature is outside. Be sure the air is blowing from the indicated vents. On vehicles that are equipped with automatic temperature control, test both the *high* and the *low* temperature in the full auto mode. Note any failure of the fan speed changes that should occur. Finally, set the temperature control to your favorite comfort level and let it run.

A simple test of the power windows is to operate both sides simultaneously. Both windows should raise and lower smoothly and at the same speed. Try them a few times. Be sure to check the back windows also. Test the function of all windows from each outboard seat even if they aren't powered.

This is also a good time to inspect the interior of each area. Feel the carpet for dampness, especially in the lowest areas of the floorboard. A vehicle with a water leak will mildew and stink forever. You might try a few sheets of those scented fabric softeners you put in the clothes dryer, under the seats. They do wonders to make a vehicle smell fresh.

Test the power seats and recliners. They should respond from full *fore* to full *aft,* and up and down, without binding or stopping in any position. Be sure to check them with and without your weight.

If the vehicle doesn't have power seats, check all stops along the track. Sometimes a heavy person may have damaged the track causing the seat to not lock in place properly. A sudden surprise movement of the seat while driving could cause an accident or loss of control.

Now that the vehicle's engine has warmed sufficiently, you should check the transmission dipstick with the engine running. Be certain the vehicle is in park and the parking brake is set firmly.

> **CAUTION! If you are wearing a necktie or have any loose or dangling clothing, remove it while you are inspecting the engine compartment.**

The automatic transmission fluid should be clear with a red tint with no other color being acceptable. Should you find the fluid pink and milky, or foamy, it is an indication of water in the transmission. This is a major problem and you should find a repair shop immediately. You may find a little black or grey fine dirt-like material floating on the dipstick in the fluid. This is an indication of clutch wear or lack of proper maintenance. If, when you drive the vehicle it seems to shift smoothly and operate properly, and there was not an excess of the clutch material on the dipstick, you should require a transmission service.

A manual transmission is difficult, if not, almost impossible, to check in this manner. It's best to check it while driving. It will either shift or not shift. Be concerned if it seems to be "*jumping*" out of gear, and grinding between shifts may indicate a problem with your synchronizers.

While under the hood with the engine running, check the power steering fluid level. If it is low, there is a leak. It should appear the same as the transmission fluid. Sometimes it is blue rather than red. At idle, there should be no grinding noises coming from the power steering pump.

Look for any fluid leaks dripping or *oozing* from any engine compartment component. Make a note of any observed abnormalities. Check the hoses; they should not appear wet or expanded around their clamps. If they do, they will require replacement soon. This will not be very costly. If the engine compartment is dusty but not greasy, you may be looking at a good engine.

Look for signs of a rusty film under the hood. This is an indication of a leaking or blown hose, or a defective radiator cap and a rusty coolant system. Most vehicles have a *coolant recovery system*. There should be coolant in the reservoir and, as a rule, it should be green in color. If it is nasty looking brown or clear, it's time for a cooling system flush. I recommend having this done professionally. Most mechanics will have a pressure tester that can spot other problems.

Scalding steam and boiling fluid can blow out of the radiator when opened, even when it is only warm. I DO mean to scare you. It can result in serious burns. I've seen it happen dozens of times.

**WARNING! Do not open the radiator cap when the radiator is the least bit warm.**

When the radiator is completely cool, you may *carefully* remove the radiator cap. If the coolant is not green and relatively clear, the vehicle needs a *cooling system flush.* This is minor, but it is an indication of poor maintenance of the vehicle. *Shame on you!*

Observe the wiring harnesses in the engine compartment. The factory usually wraps them very well. If the wires appear cut, spliced or in any disorder, they may have been repaired by a less-than-qualified technician. Ask to have them cleaned up at your next visit to the shop. A non-insulated, loose wire could *arc* to the chassis and cause component failure or worse, a *FRIED computer.* **BIG BUCKS!**

Go to the tailpipe of the vehicle. On a warm day the exhaust should be barely visible. There should not be blue or white billowy smoke coming out, an indication of oil burning. It should also not appear to be steamy. This is an indication of a defective head gasket where water is getting in the combustion chamber. Take a stiff piece of paper or a crisp dollar bill and hold it firmly to the tailpipe end while the motor is running.

The exhaust should constantly blow the paper away from the tailpipe. If it pops back and forth, or if it sucks the paper into the tailpipe (*hope you didn't use a hundred*), there is an indication of one or more burned valves in the engine. Your paper should not be oily. It is normal to have a little dry carbon apparent. It should also not be wet unless the car was just washed, or it is very cold when you are performing this test, or it has a leaking head gasket. These concerns should be reported to your repair shop for immediate repair. The mechanical problems that cause most of the above-mentioned abnormalities tend to multiply and become more costly if neglected. Fix them while they are still minor.

## TEST DRIVE

Now you are ready to test drive the vehicle. A quick jaunt around the block at 30 miles per hour doesn't tell you anything. You should try to observe your vehicle in as many driving situations as possible:

Driving on a bumpy road, idling at a stop light, take off from a stop, sudden stop, entering a freeway, passing, cruising at highway speeds, try hard turns in both directions, deceleration with light brake pressure, turning into a parking lot with an incline, parallel parking, backing up and turning hard in both directions and any other situations you can think of should be included in your test drive.

On your test drive you should turn off the radio and *listen* to your vehicle. Pops, squeaks, rattles, knocks, grinding, roars and any noises should be noted. Roll the windows down to listen. Roll them up and listen. A noise not sounding right, probably isn't. It's usually worth looking into.

Make note and observe your vehicle's *handling characteristics* and ride of the vehicle in all situations. Check the vehicle for pulling in either direction. Be aware that most roads are crowned and most vehicles will naturally drift to the right with your hands off the steering wheel. If the vehicle makes noise or shudders while braking, you can suspect the brake rotors are in need of repair. The expense of this repair varies greatly by vehicle. Either check a few places for prices, or take it to your automotive specialist you trust.

*CAREFULLY LISTEN TO AND FEEL THE SHIFT POINTS OF THE TRANSMISSION.* If it seems to wind up prior to engaging in any gear, you should be concerned about the transmission. On any vehicle with an automatic overdrive transmission, it is not uncommon to feel a positive clunk between third and fourth gear. This is normal.

It is not normal for a shift of the gears to be harsh (jerks when changing gears, it should be smooth) at any time except passing gear on hard acceleration. Observe the downshifts while you decelerate under a light brake. When shifting from *park* to any gear (particularly rear-wheel-drive vehicles), a slight clunk is often normal. This is usually referred to as *drive line slack*. If it seems to be abnormal, it could be. If there are any other vibrations or noises present on engagement, it could be any number of things including: *rear axle, universal joints, motor mounts, constant velocity joints*, or *transmission mounts* just to mention a few, any of which could get very expensive if not attended to soon. What's worse, you or your significant other and your children could be stranded in the worst possible place at the worst possible time.

After performing these simple tests, you should have a good idea as to the road readiness of your car. You should also have written a (hopefully short) list of possible concerns. "Concerns" are what most repair facilities prefer to call your automobile's "problems."

If you still like the car and decide not to get a new one, you should be almost ready to choose a repair shop. Before you go there, let me first give you some examples of a few common problems along with their likely diagnosis:

♦       *When I start my car in the morning, or after it has been sitting for six or seven hours, the engine makes a ticking noise that goes away when the car warms up.*

This is more than likely an older engine that has not had the engine oil serviced at the correct interval. The oil used may have been cheap in quality and a varnish-like build up has partially stopped up the lifters for the engine valves. The noise will, over a long period, cause the camshaft some damage. There is a possibility that an *IMMEDIATE* oil change with a quality oil may stop this problem. Also, changing your oil more frequently may prevent this from reoccurring.

## THINGS THAT GO THUMP

♦    *While driving my car I hear a constant squeal when I press the brake pedal. What is that?*

The front brake pads have a warning device that squeals when the brakes are applied. This tells you to replace the front brake pads soon, and check the rear brakes too.

♦    *I drive a 1988 ford F-150. The front wheels are always coated with dust and have a fishy odor.*

Your vehicle has *phenolic plastic brake caliper pistons,* and they are sticking. The result of this will be the loss of gas mileage from the constant brake drag. Your brakes will need replacing sooner than expected.

You could also overheat your rotors and warp them. This can get expensive if you don't attend to it quickly.

It could cost as little as $150 or as much as $800-900 if the calipers, brake rotors, brake drums or master cylinder needs to be replaced.

◆   *As I drive, the front end pulls left or right as I brake and, at times, the rear brakes feel like they don't work at all.*

Most people will ignore a brake problem until it comes to almost having an accident. If your vehicle has the above problem, the worn rear brakes may have overworked the front brakes and, depending on the road surface, may cause a pull to the left or right. You might find you can't stop the vehicle as quickly as expected.

◆   *In damp weather the rear brakes grab.*

Many rear brakes are often "drum" brakes, the predecessor of "disc" brakes. Brake *dust* builds up in the normal use of this type of brakes. If grease leaks out of the bearing seals, or brake fluid leaks out of the rear wheel cylinder, the mixture will make the rear brakes grab in rainy weather, thus creating a sliding condition. *Oops!* Look out, fender bender city.

*My front end shakes when I brake and I almost lose control on a rough road.*

With 60-70% of total vehicle weight on the front end, a worn set of struts or shock absorbers can cause your vehicle to bounce uncontrollably. Slick pavement and bad shocks spell an accident!

♦ *As I turn left or right, I hear a popping noise in my front end.*

The front end of this auto may have worn out the *upper or lower ball joints* and maybe the *steering tie-rod ends.* A loose part will cause a steering pull, popping noise, sloppy steering, uneven tire wear, and a left or right brake pull when stopping. This is most common on larger vehicles.

♦ *As I turned into my driveway, I heard a series of clicking noises that comes from each front wheel.*

If you hear this, you must be driving a front wheel drive car. Sixty percent of all autos are front wheel drive. This noise is the clicking of a *drive axle CV* (constant velocity) joint and it needs service NOW before it breaks and results in a costly repair.

If you re-pack the CV joint before it's too late, the grease and boot (rubber cover), and labor will be around $110 per axle. Since there are two axles, a pair might cost around $300. If an axle is bad the cost will almost double for each axle.

    *As I drove over some railroad tracks, I heard a banging noise in the rear end.*

There are several possibilities—one is the exhaust system. A broken hanger or a rubber bushing will cause the noise. However, if you hear an exhaust leak also, you could have a bad exhaust pipe or muffler that might be loose and could hit the underside of the vehicle.

We repaired a muffler on a 1990 Lincoln Town car. That muffler had hit the brake line and made the brakes inoperable. This could be a scary thing in heavy traffic.

    *When I get into my vehicle and try to turn the key, it's sometimes very hard to get the key to turn.*

If you put the front wheels in a bind when you parked, the steering wheel lock will press hard against the key lock in the steering column. Force the steering wheel either to the left or right (whichever is the easiest) as you turn the key. It will free up the key lock and the car will start easier.

♦    *When I tried to start my car, sometimes the starter only clicks; sometimes it starts.*

The starter is the small electrical motor that turns the engine over and lets it start. The clicking noise heard is the *solenoid* closing. It could be due to age or a poor quality solenoid. Sometimes, it does not activate the starter motor. You should also check all battery cables for fraying or damage. If they are damaged, replace them. Don't try the cheap $2.95 replacement terminals. You get what you pay for. Clean the terminals and battery posts and then tighten the connections. You might even have to replace the cables or the starter motor.

♦    *My car seems to be bleeding all over my driveway. What do I do?*

Fluid leaks can be identified by their color, their smell, and by the way they feel. Once you can identify the source of the leak, it might be only a matter of tightening a bolt to correct the problem. Try putting some white paper under the car to catch the drips and examine the texture, odor, and color.

Read on and maybe I can help you identify potential minor problems before they become major ones.

◆     *I noticed a puddle of green liquid on my garage
       floor. Is that normal?*

This could be a cooling system leak coming
from one or more of many hoses, connections, the
radiator or the engine assembly. It indicates that a
potential *overheating problem* could exist. Cars are not
designed to leak cooling system fluid on the ground at
all. Any antifreeze leaks should be taken care of
immediately. It could result in an overheating of the
engine, causing major damage and a very costly
repair. By the way, antifreeze is very tasty to your dog.
Dogs have been known to lap antifreeze and this can
cause blindness, kidney failure or even death to the
dog. Small children think it tastes good, too. Don't
leave any containers of coolant accessible. Go visit a
repair shop about this problem.

◆     *Is that thick, brown puddle oil? Should I be con-
       cerned?*

Yes! That brown puddle of thick fluid could be
engine oil. It's oily to the touch and when cold, has the
consistency of honey. If it *looks like* oil, and *feels* like
oil, it probably **is** oil. Motor oil should not be leaking
out of your car by any great amount. There is also a
possibility of leaking rear axle grease which is just a
thick, thick oil. You can probably pick it up. This "thick"

oil (grease) will most likely be leaking in the center rear of your car between the rear wheels. We'll discuss this later. Nonetheless, *All* oil leaks can and should be stopped.

A few random drops on the ground would not signal a major engine problem as much as a *puddle* of oil of any size. All vehicles, eventually, will drip or leak oil as gaskets shrink with age and sometimes bolts loosen with vibration. It only becomes absolutely necessary to worry about the leak if fresh small puddles are noticed every time the vehicle is shut off.

♦     *I saw a puddle of red liquid in the driveway after I backed out this morning. What do you think that is?*

Red fluid is usually a sign of a transmission leak and will only get worse unless taken care of. You can add transmission fluid to keep you moving until a repair professional can properly service your vehicle's transmission. On some cars, it could also be power steering fluid. If you hear a *growling* coming from your power steering pump, you need repair soon. Filling the pump will stop the noise, but not the problem.

♦     *My station wagon leaks clear fluid, should I be worried?*

A clear fluid on the garage floor could be one of

a few possibilities. If the fluid is oily to the touch and has a *mineral spirits* odor, it could be a brake fluid leak from the brake system which is a **very dangerous** situation. ***Don't drive*** . . . call a tow truck. This is an *emergency* and your vehicle should be considered inoperable. Your car may start and run but that's only half of its job; you have to be able to depend on it stopping without the aid of another object, such as another car, telephone pole, 18-wheeler, etc.

If the fluid is clear, has no odor, and doesn't feel oily to the touch, and you had your air conditioner on *prior* to parking your vehicle, it could be only conden-sation coming from the air-conditioning system. It is water coming from a tube that's meant to drain under the car. This is quite normal, especially on a humid day. If it doesn't drain there it will drain on your carpet on the passenger side. If your carpet feels moist, have the repair shop clear the *evaporator drain*. Not only will the carpet and pad mildew and stink, your *evaporator core* will corrode and leak refrigerant (*EXPENSIVE*).

Condensation does NOT come out on your tires, though. That's probably from a neighborhood dog and may be clear to golden in color. No repair necessary.

♦       *What is that thick, dark substance under my car?*

A green tinted or light grayish slippery sub-stance on a garage floor that smells very pungent is a fluid that leaks out of front or rear axles and manual transmissions. It will ruin your clothes and make your car stink if you get it inside. Get an inspection to find the source of the leak and have it corrected.

♦     *There's a blue-colored leak I noticed that smells like alcohol. Could you explain?*

A light-blue fluid that smells of alcohol indicates a leak in your *windshield washer reservoir*. This can be a dangerous situation if those little black "Love Bugs" are out and you attempt to clean your windshield while driving and you discover that all your washer fluid is gone. Constant leakage probably means leaking hoses between nozzles and reservoir or a crack in the reservoir. Easy to fix.

♦     *Something that leaked on my floor smells like rotten eggs. Help!*

A white spot with foaming acid smelling of rotten eggs is an indication that your battery is leaking acid. Any contact with this substance could result in skin burns, ruined clothing, or other health problems. If your skin comes into contact with it, rinse with water immediately. *Baking soda mixed with water* put on the floor will neutralize the acid. As a rule, you will proba-bly need a new battery.

♦     *Is it dangerous if my car leaks gasoline?*

**Yes! Yes! YES!** A gasoline leak could result in an explosion or fire since your water heater at home is usually located in the garage. A fuel leak is *the* most important leak to take care of. The most common way of finding that leak is by noticing an *odor* of gasoline around your vehicle. Don't drive it. Rather, PUSH your vehicle outside, leave the garage door open and shut off the power to your garage, especially the water heater. Call a tow truck immediately. Several people told me that they were able to fix the leak themselves. TWO who tried and didn't are now in heaven.

♦     *My car won't start? What's wrong?*

Does the engine make the sound of *trying* to start, but it doesn't? If the answer is *yes,* then you are either out of gas, or there is no spark from the ignition. There's no need to check your battery, you have power. "If it has gas and fire, it'll start!" First, check the fuel level on your gauge. If it registers enough fuel for your vehicle to start, then check for spark plug ignition.

This is simple to do by removing a wire from the spark plug and inserting the metal tip of a plastic handled screwdriver in the spark plug wire end. Hold this screwdriver near a piece of metal on the engine, and have someone else try to start the engine and see if a bright blue spark flashes between the screwdriver and the metal object on the engine that you placed the screwdriver next to. Be sure to **not** use the metal of an exposed carburetor or try this anywhere near the battery. An explosion could result.

If a bright blue spark jumps from screwdriver to object, you have an ignition spark, and the engine should start if fuel is present in the motor.

Some vehicles have a *fuel cutoff switch*. Check your owner's manual for the location of a fuel cutoff switch, especially if you hit a speed bump (sometimes called "sleeping policemen") or other object just before parking. It is designed to *trip* and shut off the electronic fuel pump in case of an accident. I've known of many $57.50 tow truck bills having to be paid when all that needed to be done was to push a button in the trunk or under the dash.

Depending on your mechanical knowledge, you may be able to repair the vehicle if no spark is present by replacing the cap, rotor, and wires but it may be wiser to let a repair professional do it. Blindly replacing unneeded parts could get expensive and might not remedy the problem. By knowing this information, you'll be able to help your mechanic diagnose the problem. He'll be very impressed, I promise, if you are able to inform him that, "I have ignition spark," or "No, I do not."

If the engine does not turn over while attempting to start the car, check the battery cables to see if they are loose or heavily corroded. If they're loose or dirty looking, clean the battery terminal and cable ends with a wire brush and reinstall, tightening correctly. If heavy corrosion is present, use baking soda and water (about two tablespoons per eight ounces of water and mix thoroughly) and pour slowly over the terminals. Be careful, this will foam and stain your driveway. (Some people use regular *coke.*) It works too!

You should still clean the terminals and cable ends with a wire brush even after the baking soda treatment. You can get a terminal cleaning tool for a couple of bucks at an auto parts house. It makes it really easy and does an excellent job. Good tool to have in the trunk with your jumper cables.

Wash the battery with cool, clean water and attempt to start the vehicle. If it still doesn't turn over, you can put a *trickle charger* on the battery and allow three to four hours to recharge battery.

You can also *jump-start* your vehicle. Get a good pair of jumper cables with six to eight-gauge wires. Don't even try the cheap ones. It's like trying to hammer with a needle. Make sure they're plenty long —at least 12 feet so you will have sufficient length to hook up two cars. Make sure the cars don't touch when trying to jump-start and that the ignition switch is *off* and both cars are in *park!* Connect one positive (red) jumper cable end to the weaker car's positive terminal. Clamp the other red clamp to the stronger car's positive (+) terminal being careful not to let the clamps touch any part of the body of the car or it will give you a slight jolt.

**The gasses released from the charging battery are very explosive!**

Now clamp the negative (black) jumper cable end to the negative terminal (-) of the stronger car and clamp the other end to a solid, immobile metal part of the weaker car's engine. You do not attach the other negative end to the weaker car's battery since this might cause an explosion from the sparks that may fly. I don't mean to frighten you with this but, be careful.

Now start the engine of the stronger car. After a minute or so, try to start the weaker car. If it doesn't start, turn off both cars and try again.

If it does start, take the jumper cables off in this way: first remove the **negative cable** from the **weaker** car's metal part, then take off the **negative cable** from the **stronger car.** Second, take off the **positive cable** from the **stronger car**, and finally take off the **positive cable** of the **weaker car**.

If the vehicle starts and runs, has it checked by a repair professional to make sure the alternator is charging correctly and the battery is in good shape.

Interior or trunk lights left on, or a door left partially open for several hours, can cause a battery to run down overnight. A burglar alarm is bad about this too. If this is a constant problem, have a professional check this situation out. My publisher friend (editor of this book) with the Mercedes had a battery continually going dead. He replaced it, and in days, it too went dead. He replaced it again; same thing. Wanting to fix the problem himself, he looked for HOURS, checking the lights at night and the burglar alarm. Still, within days, the battery was dead.

Cliff Evans, the coauthor of this book, thought about it for a few minutes and opened the trunk. He found that the radio antenna mechanism was faulty. He disconnected it and the problem was solved. So, my publisher made a stop off at the bank, then bought a new power antenna assembly (about $150).

Sudden cold weather and high temperatures can cause a battery to fail in a short period of time. Good battery maintenance, for example, like checking the water levels at least once a month (if filler caps are the removable kind) will help the battery last longer and not leave you stranded.

Americans love their cars but do not LIKE car repairs. According to the National Automotive Pars Association (NAPA), Americans would rather fill out their TAX RETURNS than take their cars to a repair shop.

Car problems, according to *Murphy's Law*, usually occur when you're late for a very important meeting, when you're all dressed up, or when the weather is cold and rainy.

Batteries will give you a warning by inconsistent starting, slow turning over of an engine and having to be jump-started from time to time. Replace it now. I recommend *Interstate* Batteries since they've been ranked between number one and five in recent battery tests of the top ten batteries. They have a real good national *no—hassle warranty* system.

♦     *What could be wrong if my car starts but makes a rattling noise?*

You could possibly have low oil level in the engine, dirty oil in the engine, or you could have a high-mileage, worn-out engine. If the oil pressure gauge stays very low once the engine is started cold, or the red oil pressure warning light flickers, shut the engine off. Allow a couple of minutes or so for the oil to drain back to oil the pan. Open the hood and check the oil level as I told you about earlier.

If the oil is very dirty, or if it has been 3,000 miles or more since you've had your oil changed, then follow the owner's manual recommendations for your vehicle for the type and weight of oil.

I like *Castrol* 20w50 if the temperature is 65° or higher, and 10w30 if the temperature is 65° or below.

**Do** follow the recommendations in your owner's manual. The manufacturer designed the engine with flow characteristics of the motor oil based on a specific viscosity. The wrong oil could damage your engine, especially if you have a turbo-charged engine.

If the oil appears to be okay or if you've recently changed the oil, check the outer perimeter of the engine and engine belts (with the engine running) for any loose objects or parts. Don't place your hands or clothes even **near** the rotating belts, fan or pulleys since they can draw you into the engine, severely injuring you. If the weather is cold when you open your hood to check a rattle or noise, you may be shocked to find a neighborhood cat all ground up by your fan as the source. They crawl up by the radiator to keep warm. Again, depending on your experience, the rattle or any loose objects may or may not be repairable by you but at least you'll be ahead of the curve when you contact your mechanic.

◆      *What if my car smokes?*

Actually, you could have a very serious problem depending on the vehicle's make, model, age, and mileage. A sticking choke making the engine run too rich, a dirty set of fuel injectors, a blown head gasket, or a very tired worn out gas-consuming engine. Pay attention to the following paragraphs and try to determine which color of smoke you see coming from your vehicle. This will indicate which type of problem you have.

A DARK GRAY or BLACK cloud of smoke coming from your exhaust pipe when the engine is cold could be either a stuck choke, or an over injecting set of fuel injectors causing the engine to run rich. This will eventually result in internal damage and poor fuel mileage that require more frequent tuneups.

A wise couple of dollars spent now could save thousands. You may be able to correct the choke problem by cleaning the choke with carburetor cleaner but most fuel injection problems will require a trained professional to properly repair it.

A LIGHT BLUE puff of smoke at start up (i.e. Hondas, Toyotas, Chevy V-8's, Ford V-8's, Chrysler V-6's) could indicate a worn set of *valve stem seals* which requires major engine repair. The light blue smoke could also be caused by a set of *worn piston rings* and would require a total overhaul of the engine. A temporary stopgap measure could be the use of heavier weight oils (standard 30 or 40 weight) and the introduction of an oil enhancement like STP oil treatment, *Restore* (oil treatment), or similar products. This will help *slow the oil consumption down,* but will not stop it from burning oil. It will, however, allow you time to save money for a very expensive engine overhaul.

A WHITE CLOUD of smoke (beyond the usual cold start vapor that a cold engine produces) could be a *blown head gasket.* This condition is a severe internal overheat indicator which usually is preceded by an engine overheating on the day before. The white smoke will have a sweet odor or smell like antifreeze. It will usually create a rough idle or engine miss as the engine attempts to run and a huge white cloud of smoke that follows you as you drive. Stop your car! Or, an internal engine meltdown and total engine failure is likely and this results in (you guessed it) thousands of dollars for repairs.

*DON'T drive your car if you see this.* Don't make it to the next exit or your hair appointment. Pull over immediately and call a tow truck. Invest fifty bucks in a tow truck to save you a couple thousand or more.

## TIRES—TIRES—TIRES

♦ *While driving on a flat smooth road, my car wants to pull to the right at all times. What could be wrong?*

All cars and trucks are properly aligned to the manufacturer's original specifications at the time of assembly and must stay within those specifications throughout their useful life. A vehicle that changes and begins to pull left or right or develops a "soft" steering may be in need of an alignment. This can only be checked by a qualified technician with an expensive alignment machine.

An easy way to determine if you have front-end problems is to take an accurate tire gauge and check all four tires for the correct tire manufacturer's air pressure. This will give you a starting base that will eliminate false impressions due to something as simple as low tire pressure.

Next, take your hands, put them at the top of each tire and, *gently,* bring your hands down while feeling the tire tread for any sharp rubber edges, smooth bald places, or large lumps in the tire tread. Before doing this motion, check the tire and make sure there is no glass, pieces of rock, or possible steel tire cord protruding from the tire tread.

Repeat the tire tread rubbing motion two or three more times, and each time be on the alert to a sharp edge on the rubber or uneven bumps. If these items are noted on the tire, several things can cause these conditions.

Other than rotating your tires (front to rear on the same side) or adding or subtracting air pressure, the average person can do nothing else without extensive training or expensive equipment. If you know the condition of your tires *before* the car is taken to a repair professional, you are less likely to be ripped off by an overzealous service salesperson or a dishonest automotive repair shop.

There's no real hard or fast rule as to when your vehicle should have its alignment checked or reset. Only a driver aware of how the vehicle performs and feels will be able to notice slight changes in the way the vehicle steers or travels down the road. A steering problem will be very gradual unless the power steering is to totally fail at one time or you strike a curb or large hole in the road knocking the car out of alignment. Also, be aware that most all roads are *crowned,* and your car may naturally want to drift to the right even with properly aligned tires.

A slight shake in the front end, a steady pull to either side, or vehicle wandering from lane to lane is something the driver would notice and immediate action should be taken to prevent the accelerated wear to the front tires. Most vehicles should have their alignment checked every 25 to 30 thousand miles, or at the installation of new tires, struts, or shocks.

Many people want to know how long tires last and why should they rotate and balance them. A tire that costs you $25.00 at a mass marketer is not going to last as long as a top quality tire would. A *Michelin radial* on the same car will last longer provided you aren't talking about a performance tire. High speed rated performance tires are soft and wear out very quickly. An *Acura NSX's* tires last only 6,000 miles if you're lucky. And, they are very expensive.

Barring accidents or objects that are run over in the course of a tire's lifetime, the cheaper tire will wear out sooner, develop cord separations, and show signs of weather cracking sooner than a more expensive tire. Whether your tires are good quality or somewhat cheaper, one way to extend their life is to have the tires rotated and balanced at least every eight to 10 thousand miles.

On *front wheel drive* cars, it is very important to rotate the tires sooner than eight thousand miles because the front tires not only *steer* the car, but also *pull* the vehicle. This causes greater wear on the front tires than the rear tires that only carry the weight of the vehicle. Uneven tire wear can also cause the car to steer and brake differently on changing, wet, or snowy road surfaces.

The best way to replace tires is to **replace an entire set** at one time. The second best way is to replace the two **front** steering tires with new ones. Look at the remaining tires, pick the tires with the best and deepest tread and put them on the rear. Never mismatch tire brands or tread patterns especially on vehicles equipped with ABS. In certain braking situations, mismatched tires could cause uneven or a loss of, traction. Be safe.

You should have your tires balanced also. A wheel balance 30 years ago was called a *bubble* balance; 20 years ago it was called a *high-speed* or *spin* balance; 10 years ago it was a *computer* balance, as it is today which allows tires to be balanced almost to a perfect condition.

This gives you greater tire wear and a very smooth ride. An out-of-balance tire can cause a vibration in the vehicle that wears out the shock absorbers and suspension parts sooner as a result of the constant vibration.

Better shops now balance tires by using a very sophisticated *computer-operated* balancing machine that tells the technician the position and weight that the tire needs to make it operate smoothly at all speeds. Most people are pleasantly surprised at how smoothly their car rides after balancing all four wheels. Most high quality tires will hold a balance much longer than cheaper tires since the tread wears slower and smoother on a better tire.

As a side note, be careful where you get the compressed air for your tires. There are many poorly maintained air compressors and tanks that can have large quantities of water in them. Water in your tires causes an unbalance; almost impossible to find. In freezing conditions, this water will freeze and wreak *havoc*.

Use your thumb or the valve cap to "bleed" the *air chuck* before airing up your tires. If a quantity of water squirts out, go somewhere else to get air.

If you do get water in your tires, and the car begins to vibrate, have the tires and rims separated at a tire store. They can remove the water from inside the tires. Be sure to have them balance your tires again.

Check for a *tread wear bar indicator* on your older, worn tires. Many years ago, the government and tire manufacturers agreed upon a uniform way of checking how much tread was left on a tire that was safe to use. The "old school" taught you to take a penny and stick it between the tread rows and if

Lincoln's head could be seen, then the tire was safe for highway use. The new way is a wear bar which runs perpendicular to the tread rows. It indicates the depth of the tread by showing a smooth flat area between the tread bars. Most state vehicle inspections have a requirement that if two or more of these tread bars can be seen in a row, the tire must be replaced.

*What people believe to be the most important items to have in you car:*

*69%--cell phone*
*22%--jack and tire tools*
*5%--flashlight*
*2%--jumper cables*
*2%--tire inflator or air pump*

# Chapter 4

# How to Choose a Shop

Let's say you've decided you can't repair the old family *funster* yourself and it's time to take her to a real professional. Now, what do you do? Let's start with some **common sense rules** and hope, that in the rush to get going again, you'll take some time to be a satisfied customer, not a plaintiff in a lawsuit.

♦   *If you are new in town or have not had to seek competent auto repair in your area before, ask a friend, co-worker, church member, neighbor, or anyone you trust where they take their automobile for quality automotive service work and if they are satisfied.*

♦   *Drive by the shop and look at its appearance. Does it look clean and neat? That's a good start. If you can, stop by between 5:00 P.M. and 6:00 P.M. Most people pick up their cars then. If there are a lot of customers screaming and cursing, this might not be the right shop for you.*

♦   *If you're a female and rude looks or wolf whistles embarrass you as you get out of your car, maybe you should seek service somewhere else.*

♦    *Look at the shop and get a feel for its being clean. Are there orderly and sharp looking well-dressed uniformed employees who look busy?*

♦    *Check out the service areas—do they look full of cars or trucks that are modern and just off the road for repair or are they old project cars that have no headlights, doors, or dust covered which indicates that the shop is not really busy.*

♦    *How are you greeted? Are they friendly, or are you being ignored and feel that you are interrupting someone's coffee break?*

♦    *Is the waiting area clean and neat or do you have to look at the floor to avoid the girly calendars that tool companies give out?*

♦    *Ask to see the **certifications** of the technicians. Good mechanics are proud of their certifications and post them conspicuously. ASE certifications, which stands for Automotive Service Excellence mean their technicians have passed the rigorous tests in the area listed on the certificate. Examples: Trim and Electrical, Air Conditioning, Transmission, Brakes, Suspension and Steering, Electronic Engine Control, Basic Ignition, etc.*

Make sure the shop's technicians are certified in areas such as engine repair, automatic transmissions, manual drive trains and axles, electronic engine performance (the computers in your car), electrical, trim, suspension, steering, brakes, heating and air conditioning.

It's important that the mechanics be certified in more than just brakes, suspension and steering. Those two are good certifications but are also the easiest to get and doesn't necessarily make someone a qualified enough *tech* to fix a highly complicated, late model car.

Good shops are proud of these, hard to come by, certifications and should display them on the walls of the office. Look for them.

◆     *Look around as you walk in the door. Does the shop have a computer for its records? Is there a computer for the mechanics to use? Are the walls adorned with achievements of the staff? Is the coffeepot on? Yes, yes, yes, yes, GOOD!*

While these items are only suggestions, let your sixth sense either keep you as a customer or send you out the door and down the road. If you are the least bit uncomfortable, don't stay there. Make the shop personnel explain the needed repairs and if you want, ask for the old parts as proof that the parts were, in fact, replaced. A good shop will have them in a bag for you to see. By being an informed and question-asking consumer, you put the shop on alert that you are looking and listening with your brain, not emotions.

However, don't go into the shop with a chip on your shoulder. Good repair shop employees and owners are well trained and dedicated people that go to church, have children in local schools, attend PTA meetings, and support the local community. Most are people just like you. If there is a problem with your repair, tell them and allow them to make it good. A quality shop will. Even the best repair shop can make a mistake. By buying this book you have taken the first step to do your part in helping prevent them.

Be absolutely certain that they understand what the symptoms are of your car **before** leaving it for service. And make certain that you read the repair order **before** you sign it and be sure that what you said is on the ticket. Don't accept a cryptic note that you don't understand. Assert yourself. You will be far less likely to be disappointed with the repairs. A good understanding makes everlasting friends.

**Before** you leave your vehicle, find out their *hourly* rate and whether there will be a "check out charge." Some shops add this in when they *diagnose* your problem and give you an estimate. Some shops have a minimum of a half hour to an hour. Most will not charge for a "check out" if you authorize them to perform the repair. It's frustrating for them to tear down a vehicle, check parts and call to quote only to hear, "No thanks. I'll buy one and put it on myself."

Always request a firm estimate **before** final authorization is given and any work is begun. If you agree to pay their estimated price ask, "Will this be the entire cost to repair my car?" If you get an "I'm not sure," you need to fully understand *why* before you give authorization. There should be very few instances where they can't be sure it will be repaired to your satisfaction at their quoted price.

If for any reason you aren't comfortable with the explanations you are given, cut your losses, refuse to authorize the repair, pay the check-out charge and find another shop. There are a lot of quality shops out there, but there's good and bad in every field. I've seen many "parts swappers" that don't have the knowledge to diagnose your concern without spending your money on replacing parts until they get lucky enough to have finally replaced the bad part.

Many shops specialize in repairing *specific makes* of cars. Oftentimes, this is a very good idea, because they are more likely to have the **special tools** required to repair that make of vehicle. New car dealerships are required by their manufacturer to purchase the special tools for each new model as they become available. This is an advantage, but you will also pay a premium in an hourly rate. Sometimes this can be as much as 30 to 50% more. Dealerships also exclusively use OEM (Original Equipment Manufactured) parts, which are most always at greater cost.

There is one situation where I highly recommend the new car dealership. If your car is under a factory warranty, **use a dealership**. Most newer cars have a minimum of a three-year or thirty-six-thousand-mile (whichever comes first), complete bumper-to-bumper warranty. This means that the manufacturer pays the **entire** cost of any repair other than ordinary maintenance items.

Also, with a new car or a car which still has a warranty, be sure to ask about their coverage of the manufacturer's **power-train** and the **emissions** component warranties that often extend to five years or up to 100,000 miles (whichever comes first). Power-train warranties usually have a deductible of around $100 per occurrence, and a hundred bucks is a **lot less expensive** than a transmission or engine would cost you if you had to bear the entire cost. It's usually **thousands** of dollars.

Picking a good repair shop is difficult. With a little diligence you can usually find a good one that you can trust and depend upon. If you know something about your vehicle, you can avoid getting *stung* by a bad mechanic or a bad repair shop; **they are every-where**. Many will take unfair advantage of the unknowing. *Act* stupid, but don't **be** stupid, please.

You don't need to be a mechanic in order to not get gypped, just READ THIS BOOK and do your best to remember the important QUESTIONS to ask. Listen, ask questions and be nice.

A friend of mine has an underwater salvage business. There's a big sign in his shop and on his business card that reads:

*Estimates Vary According To*
*Customer's Attitude!*

## AUTO TECHNICIANS **BEST** CUSTOMERS

*Respect technician's time* . . . . . . . . . . . . . . . . . . . . *19%*
*Are courteous and make referrals* . . . . . . . . . . . . *16%*
*Realize vehicles are complex* . . . . . . . . . . . . . . . . *16%*
*Are loyal, repeat customers* . . . . . . . . . . . . . . . . . *15%*
*Keep up with maintenance* . . . . . . . . . . . . . . . . . *13%*
*Don't haggle over price* . . . . . . . . . . . . . . . . . . . . . *12%*
*Give gifts* . . . . . . . . . . . . . . . . . . . . . . . . . . . . . . . . *9%*

## AUTO TECHNICIANS **WORST** CUSTOMERS

*Do not respect technician's time* . . . . . . . . . . . . . . *26%*
*Do not trust technicians diagnosis* . . . . . . . . . . . . *19%*
*Do not disclose pre-existing conditions* . . . . . . . . . *18%*
*Want freebies, haggle over price* . . . . . . . . . . . . . . *17%*
*Unqualified do-it-youselfers* . . . . . . . . . . . . . . . . . *13%*
*Neglect maintenance* . . . . . . . . . . . . . . . . . . . . . . . *9%*

# Chapter 5

# Understanding Repair Charges

"How can this be? I brought my car in at 2:00 P.M. this afternoon and picked it up at 5:00 P.M. and you're charging me for **six** hours labor!" This doesn't make any sense at all. Are you getting ripped off? The answer is *no*, you're not getting ripped off, and *yes,* it is more than likely, fair. Let me explain why.

It's called "flag hours." *No*, nothing patriotic or even military, it's a system to **fairly charge** for the individual tasks done and to be consistent or uniform in the charges no matter which *tech* performed the repair or what level of experience the technician has.

There are two commonly accepted standards for flag hours. One is called "warranty time" and the other is called "Chilton time." There are others, but they are mostly variations of the same theme.

**Warranty time** is set by each manufacturer as to the hours they will pay for each task in the repair of a vehicle under warranty. They produce a book that lists every procedure for each vehicle they manufacture and the time in tenths of an hour allowed to perform the procedure. **Chilton** is a company that independently produces a guide with the same allowances for each make and model vehicle with each and every procedure possible; it's a fat book and there are many volumes.

Both the manufacturers and Chilton perform time studies to determine how many hours are allowed for each procedure. The studies are based on the *average length of time* that an *average* technician takes to perform each task with common hand tools (*NOT AIR-POWERED TOOLS*).

Time is allocated for obtaining the vehicle, putting it on a lift (if necessary), diagnosis using a shop manual, obtaining parts from an on-site location, performing the part exchange, testing the repair and returning it to the holding area. The technician will have all of the "special tools" required but, will not have access to power or air tools, only *hand* tools.

For example, it might pay 4-tenths of an hour to remove, rotate and replace four wheels. That's 24 minutes. If he has an air powered impact wrench and two good floor jacks, he can do it in less than six minutes. He still gets paid for 24 minutes. It pays to hustle. That's why you see the good technicians with those big $4,000 tool chests with $10,000 worth of tools in them. They save time which equates to money for them.

How fast a tech can average doing his work is measured in his *efficiency rating*. Technicians can run an efficiency rating of 135% or even better with quality power tools and still be doing a thorough job. That means, he can work an 8-hour day and get paid for 10.8 hours or more.

"Let's see," you say. "The guy gets **paid** for 10.8 hours in a day. I'm paying $60.00 per hour. He's making $648.00 per day!" Don't quit your job just yet to become an automotive technician.

The **shop** may charge $60.00 per hour, not the tech. The technician may only make from $10 to $20 per hour, depending on his certifications and diligence. The rest goes to cover the shop's overhead, profit and support personnel.

You, on the other hand, benefit by having a standardized system for the charges you pay no matter how long it takes or who does your work. When there is a question as to what is charged, there is an acceptable source to verify the fair price for services.

It also provides the shop manager with a "tool" to judge the quality of work performed by monitoring the efficiency rating of their technicians. Typically, a technician with an extremely high efficiency rating may be short cutting the repair procedure or occasionally charging for repairs not performed and warrants a closer look. By the same token, a tech with a low efficiency rating may not be qualified to work in an area of specialization or may need additional training.

If you feel a repair bill is a too high, ask what time standard they use and ask to see the book that tells the allowed time for your repair procedure. A good shop will post their hourly rate and the standard used.

If you noticed other charges on your repair bill or large letters like GOG, recycle fees, shop supplies, etc. What are these you ask?

They are charges that the repair facility adds to their repair bill to cover costs of doing business. GOG also known as "Gas, Oil and Grease" is a common addition to a repair order to charge you for incidental fluids, solvents, and lubricants used in your repair. If a can of WD-40 is charged as parts on your repair, there shouldn't be a GOG charge. The GOG sometimes listed as "shop supplies" is usually a small percentage of the total parts and labor charges. It averages around 1% sometimes more, sometimes less.

Recycle fees are also added to the ticket, especially when hazardous materials that are required by law to be specially handled. Oil, tires, batteries, engine coolants containing ethylene glycol, and Freon cannot be disposed of without following the guidelines of the EPA. Your shop may charge you fees for their disposal or recovery if they were required to repair your vehicle. Some of the fees are regulated by law.

The funny thing is, they charge you to reclaim the refrigerant in your air-conditioning system. And then they charge you for the same Freon they put **back** in your system. What they take out of your system goes into their supply tank. That's how the EPA set it up, they're not really doing anything underhanded.

There are a few small, one-mechanic shops that

charge straight time for their repairs. Most of them can't beat the clock time in a Chilton book. Some of them aren't Harvard graduates and straight time is all they understand. If the mechanic is good and he charges straight time, you might be getting a good deal. Only you can judge by your repair expense and the number of "*Try it again, Sam*" trips you make.

## SHOULD I DO IT MYSELF?

So you only have a hammer, a pair of pliers, a pocket screwdriver, a metric crescent wrench and a burning desire to *do it yourself*. You may not be the most mechanically inclined person in the world, but you'd like to not be *totally* helpless when it comes to dealing with your vehicle in need of a little TLC.

You see the little handle with the picture of an open hood on it, and pull. *POP!* And it springs up just far enough to let you stick your fingers in to get thoroughly dirty while finding the safety catch. *Click!* A little push down and you lift up the hood and *WOW!* There it is; the engine. A veritable maze of wires, hoses, *thingamabobs, whatchamacallits* and gadgets that you have absolutely **no idea** what they are, much less, what they do. And you ask, "Can I do it myself?"

Life is an adventure. Let's give it a try and see exactly what you **can** do. At the risk of being overly simplistic, I'm going to assume you know absolutely *nothing* about the underhood of your car. We've already discussed reading your owner's manual, so we know that you really **do** know something about what you're looking at. But to review, I'm going to resort to some graphic aids in the next chapter. I call it, "Show and Tell."

*Chapter 6*
# Show and Tell

    I first played *"Show and Tell"* in kindergarten. Now, I do it for a living. Don't be overwhelmed by the terminology used when getting that call-back from the service advisor and approve unneeded repairs not knowing what you are being told. ***ASK!***

    It is their job to fully explain what they're going to do before they perform repairs. If it doesn't make sense, don't do it, or get a second opinion. It is your money; spend it wisely

    I've included some pictures of a few common major components. That's right. We've got pictures! In this case a picture is *really* worth a thousand words. Maybe it's not your make of car, but most concepts are the same and your components will look similar. I hope this will assist you in identifying an area of a malfunction. You might be able to better communicate to a repair facility after viewing these pictures.

    Your friends and neighbors will be impressed when you tell them you know how to check the oil in a Lexus. Here's more with some additional helpful hints in the captions included:

This is a typical "alternator" which charges a battery.

This is a "Brake Fluid Reservoir" If you check your brake fluid level, **DO NOT ALLOW ANY DIRT TO GET INSIDE.**

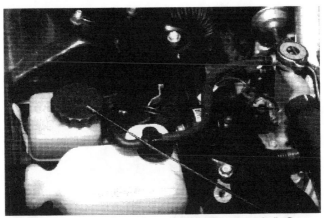

*This a "Power Steering Fluid Reservoir." Some vehicles have their reservoir built into the power steering pump which looks considerably different.*

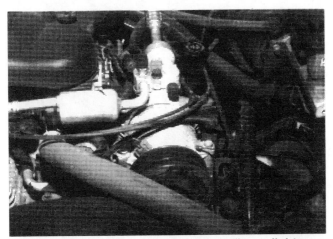

*A typical air conditioner compressor (large light grey object in center.) The tubing attached to the rear going left and back is called the "High Pressure Hose."*

*This is a "McPherson Strut" It controls up and down movement of the front suspension and absorbs shocks.*

*This is a "Serpentine Belt." They are kept tight by an automatic tensioner as they stretch with wear. "V-Belts" must be tightened occasionally.*

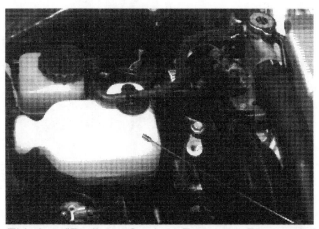

*This is a "Radiator Coolant Recovery Reservoir." If you can KEEP coolant in this reservoir at ALL times, you may not have to add coolant to the radiator.*

*This is the under view of a "Front Wheel Drive Vehicle." The transmission is called a "Trans-axle" which is on the right. The engine oil pan is on the left.*

*This is a "Fuse Box" under the hood. Some vehicles' fuse box is under the dash, some are in the glove box.*

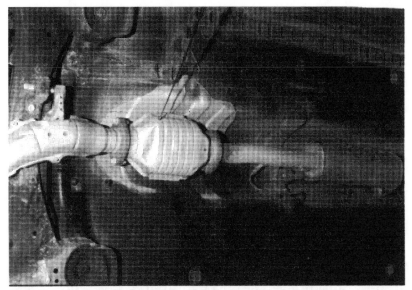

This is a "Catalytic Converter." It burns the excess hydrocarbons in the exhaust gasses. As they get older, they may get plugged (especially if your motor burns oil) and require replacement. **It could get so hot it turns cherry red. Be careful driving over tall, dry grass.**

The best thing for you to do now is to try and identify each of these components on your vehicle. Consult your owner's manual and identify the components listed in it. Congratulations! By now, you probably know as much about a vehicle as 90% of the general public. Now are you ready to learn more? Read on.

The National Institute of Automotive Service Excellence (ASE) was established in 1972. ASE's mission is to improve the quality of vehicle service and repair by testing and certifying automotive repair technicians.

Today, more than 440,000 professional technicians are ASE certified. They work in every segment of the automotive service industry: car and truck dealerships, independent garages, service stations, fleets franchises, schools, on race teams and more.

Consumers benefit from ASE certification. It is a valuable yardstick by which to measure the knowledge and skills of individual technicians as well as the commitment to professionalism and quality of the repair facility employing the ASE-certified technician.

*An excerpt from Tech News/USA Today November, 1998.*

# Interesting Q & A

I get a lot of questions on the air. Some, more often than others. The following questions are asked often and have answers that most find interesting. So, I decided to include them in this book. I feel they will help to round out your overall automotive knowledge.

## TEXAS TEA, — OIL, THAT IS

I know we've already discussed checking your oil. There are so many people that have numerous questions about oil, here's a few of their questions and answers:

**Do I need to change my engine oil and filter together, or can I change the filter every other time I do the oil?**

Some owners' manuals suggest this type of oil maintenance. Let's remember that not all manufacturers of automobiles want the engine in your car to last an indefinite time period. They call it "***planned obsolescence***." If you follow this misinformation, you leave contaminated oil, acids, moisture, dirt and debris in your engine when you do not change the oil filter and only change the oil. It is not a good idea to do this and if money is a factor, remember, most engines cost between $2,000 to $10,000 to replace. The oil filter is an inexpensive way of protecting your vehicle investment.

## Why do so many oils have such a price range?

The more **quality** a quart of oil, the more it should cost. All oils sold have ASE rating on the back of the container. The higher the rating, the better the quality of the oil. The letters "CC" indicate a good oil, but a "CF," "CG," or "CH" is even a better quality. Cheap oil is probably an oil with no "chemical packages" in the oil. These oils are good for lawnmowers and chainsaw blade lubricating, not today's high performance, very costly, and hot running automobile engines.

The quality of a motor oil is measured by its ability to withstand extreme heat and pressure. The oil molecules that make the oil very slippery, do not break down as quickly as a lower grade. Certain chemical packages are added to single viscosity oil (30w) are commonly referred to as "detergents." They actually clean inside your engine while you drive. Oil quality is also improved by chemicals like *zinc, ash, copper, lead* and *polymers* (two or more compounds). These are only in *trace amounts* in oil but these chemicals and minerals make the oil tougher.

**What is multi-grade oil versus straight weight oil?**

The weight rating on oil has reference to its *viscosity*. A straight 30 weight oil means it has a 30w viscosity—its like molasses when it is cold and like water when it is hot. When your engine is cold, you want the oil to flow rapidly to all moving parts. A 10-weight oil is thinner than a 30-weight oil. It would be great if your engine could start with a 10-weight oil. However, after 10w oil warms up, it is so diluted, it doesn't provide enough friction-bearing properties to prevent wear.

A multi-grade oil or "Multiple Viscosity Oil" (for example 10w30 or 20w50) has the viscosity character-istics of the first number when its cold and the viscosity characteristics of the second number when it's hot! The advantage of a 10w30 weight oil is that it will flow much quicker on a cold start up protecting the engine parts sooner. As 10w30 gets warmer the oil does not get as thin as a straight weight oil would. It actually gets thicker to keep the oil flowing at the level needed and maintaining oil pressure where it should be. You can't tell about this action just by looking at the oil, but your engine sure can.

## What is a cartridge oil filter?

Most modern automobiles have a screw-on cartridge oil filter that has an "O" ring as a seal on its top. A quality oil filter like this will spin on. It will require an additional ¾ turn once the o-ring is seated, no more! The filter should be removed and disposed of properly after each oil service. Do not place these in your trash. In most states it is illegal and even though the chances of being caught are remote, the damage to the environment is quite high. Most oil change places will take your filters gladly and dispose of them properly.

## What is a drop-in filter?

A drop-in filter is an old style filter that has a removable center filter element and reusable canister. When changing these filters, you will get dirty due to having to wash out the canister and handling a quart of concentrated dirty oil along with the element. Again, do not toss this filter out in the trash since it is open and will begin to contaminate the groundwater as soon as it hits the trash dump. Take a gallon milk jug, cut a corner open so the element will drop inside, and take it to an oil change store. They will be happy to recycle the element for you.

## What happens to oil if the engine overheats?

This is not an easy question to answer. I live in San Antonio which basically is on the edge of a desert, and I have seen oil turn into tar and resin due to severe overheating created by high air temperature, high speed, towing, air conditioning, or poor radiator cooling. An engine develops an enormous amount of heat as it generates power to pull your vehicle down the road. Too few oil services will also cause the oil to thicken up. If the condition is not corrected quickly, the engine will suffer a fatal internal explosion and require several thousands of dollars of work.

## Why do oil filters vary in price so much?

Remember one of the first thoughts of this book is, "Quality and cheap don't mix." An oil filter, no matter how cheap, will filter dirt and debris. Take a *Fram, AC, Delco, Purolator, Baldwin, Motorcraft, Wix,* and other name brand filters, and feel their weight compared to a no name off brand filter. The quality filters will be heavier due to more and denser filter material inside the canister. A cheaper filter change is better than no filter change and will protect somewhat. A cheap filter will allow particles of carbon, metal and varnish to bypass and act like small pieces of grinding compound inside your engine.

A quality oil filter will remove particles in the

three to seven micron range which will reduce harm to your engine. A cheap filter will allow particles up to 10 and 15 microns to pass through into your engine, creating premature wear and eventual costly repair.

**My 1989 Honda Accord is at 100,000 miles. Do I need to replace the timing belt?**

Yes, the belt has a life of 90,000 miles on the '89 Hondas. Earlier models need the timing belt replaced at 60,000 miles. If one fails, the engine is history.

**How often should I service my automatic transmission?**

Many owners' manuals say every 50,000 miles. Some say not at all. You should service most transmissions between 20,000 and 25,000 miles. If you have a towing-type vehicle, all in-town driving, and high speed, you might lower that number to 12,000-15,000 miles. The fluid should be red and not smell like shoe polish in the liquid bottle form.

**How often do I tune-up my vehicle?**

Depending on gas mileage, if you keep a good log book of miles between fill ups, you should know what your average gas mileage is. When that number falls two mpg for two consecutive tanks of similar driving, tune it up! A good rule of thumb is to tune around 25,000 to 30,000 miles. Don't believe the 100,000 between tune ups—that's for the "*NORMAL*" driving no one has ever done.

## When should I replace the belts and hoses?

My favorite answer for this is every two years or 50,000 miles. Yes, rubber hoses have improved and their life is much longer, but remember it's hard to tell when they need replacing unless it is *really* apparent (white smoke coming from under the hood.) A set of hoses are much cheaper than a new motor or a long tow behind a wrecker while on vacation.

## What is a V-belt?

Most older cars (pre-1988) have V-belts that power the different accessories under the hood of your car. The new single belted engines use a "serpentine" belt. It is wise to carry an extra set of belts in your trunk. There's nothing wrong with "*used*" spares, (not broken.) If you have your belts replaced, ask the repairman to put the old belts in the jackets the new belts came out of. Put them in the trunk with your spare tire for emergency use. Should you use it, the jacket has the replacement part number printed right on it. Aren't you smart!

☆ ☆ ☆ ☆ ☆ ☆

The present day auto does everything from keeping us cool or warm to changing the ride height and suspension needs while we drive with the relative speed of a Pentium II MMX computer. The Modern day auto has more computers on board than most military engine aircraft. And yet, we still expect them to perform well no matter what the road conditions or weather has to offer. The present day car has more stereo power than most home units and offers all this at 30 miles per gallon at 70 mph.

Luckily, the information in this book is basic enough and common to most design concepts for vehicles in the recent past, present and the fairly distant future (next 10 years). The complexities of the electronic changes should not concern you as they are the burden of your repair professional. They should be the ones you depend on to deal with the repair of the new high tech components. If they are going to stay in the industry, they will be forced to change with the technology. It is often said of the automobile business, "The only thing constant is change."

## *Good Luck with your automobiles!*

# About the Author

**Steve Gehrlein** is an automotive repair expert with over 17 years experience in auto repair and maintenance. As the host of a radio program called, *The Automotive Show* on 550AM-KTSA in San Antonio, Texas. His vast knowledge of automobiles qualifies him to answer call-in automotive questions in a talk show format.

Steve is on the technology board for North East Independent School District and as a NASCAR stock car owner, a supporter of the sport.

As a former San Antonio police officer, Steve has served as an expert witness for over 20 local law firms on automobile cases.

Additionally, he is the owner of Cambridge Auto Center, an independent professional repair facility in San Antonio, Texas.

**Cliff Evans** is the consummate car professional and has been involved in every facet of the automobile business during the past 25 years. As is a member of the Society of Professional Sales Managers, Mr. Evans has managed every department; sales, finance, service, fleet, parts, rental, leasing, the body shop and general offices, individually and collectively, in some of the largest automobile dealerships in the world.

Cliff Evans also authored a book titled, *How to Buy a New Car and Save Thou$ands,* a truly terrific book that **will** save you thousands of dollars on your next new car purchase.

*STEVE GEHRLEIN is available for personal appearances, luncheons, banquets, interviews, seminars, etc. He is entertaining and informative. Call (210) 697-9600 for cost and availability.*

☆ ☆ ☆ ☆ ☆ ☆

Send a personal check or money order in the amount of $12.85 per copy to: Swan Publishing, 126 Live Oak, Alvin, TX, 77511. Please allow 7-10 days for delivery.

## To order by major credit card 24 hours a day, seven days per week call: (281) 388-2004

☆ ☆ ☆ ☆ ☆ ☆

Libraries—Bookstores—Quantity Orders call:

### Swan Publishing
**126 Live Oak**
**Alvin, TX 77511**

**Call (281) 388-2547, Fax (281) 585-3738**
**e-mail: swanbooks@ghg.net**
**Web Page: http:\\www.swan-pub.com**
*Cliff Evans: www.autoace.org*

Distributed by Hervey's Booklink, Dallas, Texas
(214) 221-2711, Fax (214) 221-2715